Remembering

Providing support for children aged 7 to 13
who have experienced loss and bereavement

Lorna Nelson and Tina Rae

Illustrated by Simon Smith

SAGE Publications Ltd
1 Oliver's Yard
55 City Road
London EC1Y 1SP

SAGE Publications Inc
2455 Teller Road
Thousand Oaks
California 91320

SAGE Publications India Pvt. Ltd
B 1/I 1 Mohan Cooperative Industrial Area
Mathura Road, New Delhi 110 044
India

SAGE Publications Asia-Pacific Pte Ltd
33 Pekin Street #02-01
Far East Square
Singapore 048763

www.luckyduck.co.uk

Library of Congress Control Number Available

British Library Cataloguing in Publication Data
A catalogue record for this book is available from the British Library

ISBN 978-1-904315-42-1

Contents

How to use the CD-ROM

The CD-ROM contains PDF files, labelled 'Worksheets.pdf' which contain worksheets for each lesson in this resource. You will need Acrobat Reader version 3 or higher to view and print these resources.

The documents are set up to print to A4 but you can enlarge them to A3 by increasing the output percentage at the point of printing using the page set-up settings for your printer.

To photocopy the worksheets directly from this book, set your photocopier to enlarge by 125% and align the edge of the page to be copied against the leading edge of the copier glass (usually indicated by an arrow).

A note on the use of gender

Rather than repeat throughout the book the modern but cumbersome 's/he', we have decided to use both genders equally throughout the range of activities. In no way are we suggesting a stereotype for either gender in any activity. We believe that you can adapt if the example you are given does not correspond to the gender of the child in front of you!

A note on the use of the words 'family' and 'parents'

Many children do not live in conventional two parent families. Some are looked after by the local authority and might have confusing and painful experiences. We often use the term 'carer' to identify the adults who look after such a child or young person. Sometimes 'people you live with' might be more appropriate than 'family'. These phrases can make the text rather repetitive. Please use the words most suitable for the young people you work with.

Chapter I

Loss and Bereavement

Introduction

Feelings of loss are a life experience common to all of us. Such experiences touch and affect everyone, as we move through the different stages in our lives from early infancy to old age. We witness many changes within ourselves and significant others via the events of our life. Just as life is ever changing, so are our life experiences. These may include changing schools, moving home or making and losing friends. Each experience can promote a variety of emotions. Some may cause happiness whilst others facilitate less comfortable emotions which may both challenge our understanding of the world and be a cause of pain, which can be physical, emotional or spiritual (Mitchell, 1987).

'Pain can be physical, emotional or spiritual- whatever aspect it starts with, it will always spread to the others, so the earlier we start dealing with the pain of loss and death the less likely it is to affect the other aspects.' (Mitchell, L 1987 International Stress and Tension Control Annual Conference)

Like adults, children's lives are touched by an array of events, which can suggest that the movements of life provide very little stability. One of the stable features within children's lives is often the school context and the role of their teachers. Schools and teachers can help children develop their emotional understanding and their skills in the area of emotional literacy. This may include the ability to accept the changes they experience through the preparation and the development of strategies to effectively cope with change and loss.

Change and loss are intricately linked. However, what loss signifies is represented for most of us through death. It is important to note that there are many types of loss, which can also involve the expression of

5

grief, sorrow and mourning. What has been ~~~~~~ vledged is that unresolved loss can have harmful effects on both physical and psychological wellbeing. The acceptance of death, loss and bereavement is perhaps best seen as a personal journey which can lead to personal growth and development. Nevertheless, this is clearly dependent upon the nature of the loss and whether it is recognised and acknowledged.

'There is no growth without pain and conflict and no loss that cannot lead to gain.'(Pincus, L 1976)

Definitions and meanings

The words 'death', 'loss' and 'bereavement' all have specific meanings, yet at the same time they can also be defined through the personal understanding and experience of the individual. A simple and succinct definition of death can be found in the Concise Oxford Dictionary (1990) where death is defined as 'the ending of life'. However, the idea of loss is also embedded into the word bereavement which can be described as 'the loss of something that is precious'. Bereavement is a word that is usually used when describing the loss of a person. Nevertheless, the emotions and the processes can be the same as those associated with the loss of an inanimate object, a change in a particular situation or the ending of a relationship. Incorporated into the emotion of bereavement is grief, which is the emotional, psychological and physical manifestation of bereavement. For many young people their first experience of loss will be a loved family pet and this can provide a good opportunity to talk about death and experience grief and recovery.

As previously mentioned, our lives are touched by a cycle of events which continually involve change and loss. These can be defined in two categories: predictable changes and losses and circumstantial changes and losses. Predictable changes and losses are related to every aspect of life and will affect everyone, whilst circumstantial changes and losses are situational and are usually dependent upon individual circumstances.

Predictable changes and losses include growing up, going to school and changing schools. The change and the loss involved in growing up includes losing habitual patterns of earlier childhood routines and ways, gaining autonomy and developing independence from parents/carers. Going to school entails coping with separation from parents and family;moving from class to class sometimes involves developing new friendship groups and working with different teachers. The anxiety of changing schools relates to losing a familiar environment made up by surroundings, teachers and friends. All these changes and losses are a part of life and are considered to be 'expected changes'. The second type of change and loss is circumstantial and these can be classified as follows: whole-school issues that affect individuals, issues related to staff members of the school and personal issues that relate to aspects of the children's lives (Brown, 1999).

Whole-school issues that may contribute to circumstantial changes and losses are as follows:

- accident
- death of a pupil or member of the school staff
- disaster
- new school building
- staff changes
- structural damage

Circumstantial changes and losses in school staff's lives are as follows:

- accident
- changing jobs
- death of a colleague
- divorce or separation
- illness
- miscarriage
- moving house

Circumstantial changes and losses in children's lives are as follows:

- abuse
- change of house and country
- death of a family member or friend
- divorce or separation
- family breakdown
- friends and family moving away
- friendship changes
- homelessness
- illness and special needs
- imprisoned family member
- loss of self-esteem
- new siblings
- parent returning to work or losing job

The events listed above perhaps demonstrate that different aspects of life can be a trigger for individuals to experience a sense of loss or bereavement.

Effects of loss

To understand the effects of loss, it is necessary to understand the concept of attachment. *Attachment Theory* (Bowlby, 1969) underpins the concept of change and loss. Attachment Theory advocates that attachment is formed when affectional bonds with others are established and grief is the reaction when such bonds are broken or threatened.

It has been argued that attachment derives from a human need for security and safety that will extend throughout life.

'Attachment behaviour is any form of behaviour that results in a person attaining proximity to some other clearly identified individual who is conceived as better able to cope with the world.'

The patterns of attachment and the conditions which aid the development of attachment are rooted and associated with the child-parent or caregiver interaction, i.e. how the parent(s) or caregiver(s) treat and interact with the child.

There are three major patterns of attachment: 'secure', 'anxious resistant' and 'anxious avoidant'. Secure attachment means that an individual is sure that the caregiver is always available and is prepared to give help when requested. Anxious resistant attachment promotes the establishment of uncertainty, about whether the parent(s) or the caregiver(s) will be available or responsive when needed. Anxious avoidant attachment results in the individual having no confidence and not expecting the parent(s) or the caregiver(s) to be available when required.

Typical behaviour we can observe in children might be:

Secure – confident child, happy to separate appropriately and plan for future

Anxious resistant – child who is distressed at separation and anxious about friendships

Anxious avoidant – detached, making poor relationships, may be hostile.

Once bonding and attachment has been established with the caregiver, separation anxiety also develops. This anxiety relates to the 'anxiety about losing, or becoming separated from someone loved'. Bowlby explained that the concept of separation is a difficult phenomenon to conceptualise, but the important aspect to separation anxiety is the fear of loss, coupled with the actual loss.

According to Attachment Theory the bond established in early infancy and childhood with parent(s) or primary caregiver(s) is important in order to support positive emotional development and the ability to establish and maintain relationships in later life. When considering children's reactions to death, loss and bereavement it has been debated whether children's reactions are the same as adults. Studies and research into this topic have shown that children and young people grieve in the same way as adults. However, there are differences and these relate to the period of intense grief, which is considered to be shorter for children. The whole grieving process may be much longer for children than for adults. There are significant characteristics which affect whether a child or a young person copes effectively with death, loss and bereavement. These are as follows:

- age
- circumstances of the loss i.e. expected or unexpected
- developmental level
- gender
- personality
- previous life experience
- support systems in child's life.

Another area which may affect whether a child is able to cope with death, loss and bereavement is the cultural and religious background. The process of grieving may be shaped or dictated by the customs of the religion or culture.

Some children, especially refugees and asylum seekers, might have extreme circumstances of death, loss and bereavement and will also be living with perpetual uncertainty. Special support programmes will be appropriate to help these young people. (Allen, P., Warwick, I. & Begum, J. 2004)

Most common reactions

A person experiencing the loss of a loved one will have many reactions. The major and most common reactions are shock, anger, grief, sorrow, protest, numbness, disbelief and ultimately acceptance and the continuation of life.

The process of grief

The process of grief has many different dimensions and stages. These include shock, denial, growing awareness and acceptance incorporating readjustment. The first dimension and stage in the process of grief is shock. It is the initial response to major loss.

There are many ways in which shock can manifest itself. These include the following:

- lack of response
- numbness
- silence or inactivity
- physical collapse
- outburst of emotion i.e. screaming, shouting, confusion in speech
- change in behaviour.

Denial

The second stage of grief is denial. Denial is usually experienced at the onset or the early stages of loss. During this stage the individual attempts to come to terms with the loss. They may fluctuate between the reality of the situation and denial. The role of denial at this time is to provide a coping mechanism to deal with times when the individual is unable to cope with their loss and grief.

Awareness

The third dimension in the process of grief is growing awareness. This involves becoming aware of the reality of the change and loss. There are many different emotions involved such as sadness, yearning, despair, guilt, anxiety, anger and depression. During this process it is normally usual for children to look for what they have lost and they can tend to be touched by episodes of sadness. These periods of sadness are usually shorter for children than for adults. Children may not want to express their sadness and therefore may attempt to hide this from others. One of the means of coping with sadness is to find comfort in a tangible object that may belong to the person who has died or who is absent from the child's life. Children sometimes have hopes that they will be able to find what has been lost, especially those who experience the loss of a parent through divorce.

Despair

Another emotion a child may experience is the feeling of despair. This may be revealed once the child realises that they are unable to find the lost object and can be manifested in silent behaviour, withdrawal, vocalisation through screams, inconsolable tears and the rejection of affection and comfort from others.

Guilt

Guilt is an emotion that also influences a child's behaviour during this period of growing awareness. When children understand the idea that the loss is permanent they can also have feelings of remorse or guilt i.e. they feel that they are in some way responsible for the situation. Having feelings of guilt can lead to high levels of anxiety and fear. A memory of an angry outburst or an argument can provoke guilty feelings, even if the relationship was good and loving.

Anxiety

The feeling of anxiety is part of developing an understanding of the losses, especially the loss of a parent through death, separation or divorce. This can lead to increased levels of anxiety in children as they feel that their support structures and those that they've relied on for security have been taken away. They may also fear possible future loss and that the current loss may in some way be repeated. The behaviour displayed by children experiencing anxiety can be characterised by higher levels of attention seeking behaviour and sometimes can lead to school refusal.

Anger

Anger is also a common emotion felt by both adults and children after a loss. It may be demonstrated verbally or physically. Anger can be directed internally and on some occasions, anger can be directed at a person or God. There may also be anger towards the dead person, which can cause guilt.

Depression

The mixed emotions of anger, anxiety and guilt can lead to the reduction of self-esteem and eventually to feelings of depression. Depression can be characterised by extreme loneliness, despair, feelings of emptiness and worthlessness. Depression can also wipe out the importance of things which used to be of importance to children and adults and hinder the person's ability to plan ahead and think of the future.

Acceptance and readjustment

As time goes by the intense feelings of loss will decrease and the child will be able to discuss their feelings more readily and return to establishing routines. The process of acceptance and readjustment allows the bereaved to begin to participate in life.

The grief that is felt over a loss or death is not linear and people's emotions can change rapidly. The progression through the different stages of grief can be circular as unexpected events can trigger and reactivate feelings.

The grieving process can take approximately two years but this is clearly influenced by individual circumstances and contexts.

Possible reactions to grief

There are many possible reactions young children can have when dealing with the loss of a significant individual in their lives. The bereaved child may exhibit behaviour which suggests that they are in a state of shock and appear to go through daily activities mechanically and automatically. Young children can also appear to be apprehensive and experience periods of panic. Alternatively, some bereaved children can become withdrawn from their daily lives and social activities and appear to be gazing into space for long periods of time i.e. presenting as disconnected from reality. They may also be prone to misbehaving due to issues with anger as described earlier.

Like adults, the reactions of young children to a significant loss in their lives is varied. Many growing children experience the death of a family member, or close friend, but a significant number of children experience the separation of their family unit through divorce or separation. Divorce can be described as the death of a marriage and will consequently have a great impact on many young children. One in three marriages end in divorce in Britain and this is currently the highest divorce rate in Europe. The greatest victims of divorce can sometimes be the children who feel the impact of the separation for a lifetime. As the break up of the family unit is a common experience, it is therefore important for schools and teachers to be able to work effectively with children's feelings and emotions in these circumstances.

One in five children will experience the divorce of their parents before they are sixteen and half of these children will lose contact with their fathers within two years. Therefore, many children feel that they are deserted by a parent after the separation. Women will also tend to lose a significant proportion, maybe half, of their income after a divorce which means that the children consequently grow up in poorer housing with less material wealth than children in the same social class whose parents are together. Children of divorced parents find that as the years go by, especially after ten years, more than half have lost contact altogether with the parent who left the home. Pupils whose families have divorced, separated or are in the process of separating are under a great strain when also attempting to cope with everyday life. This strain may lead to a less positive attitude towards the school context.

Children who experience the divorce or separation of their parents can feel that they have little power over those who directly control their lives and therefore they can feel helpless in the situation and rejected by their parents. This is particularly true if their opinions have not been taken into consideration and they are unable to influence the changes in their lives such as relocating to a new home, a new school and losing friends due to these changes. However, schools can help children manage the changes in their lives and this publication will detail some of the support structures, systems and strategies that schools can utilise for this purpose.

Children may demonstrate signs of anxiety and stress as a result of the tension in their home lives. Teachers therefore need to be sensitive to the individual child's needs and feelings. It is important to recognise that school may be one of the most stable environments in children's lives as the parents are involved in the process of separation and divorce. It is consequently vital that teachers develop the appropriate knowledge about the impact of change, loss and bereavement on children, along side the observational skills necessary to identify those who may be currently going through the process.

Boys and girls are likely to have different responses to divorce or to the separation of the family unit. Boys can tend to be aggressive and disruptive and may get into trouble at school. They are also more prone to bedwetting, which may lead to unpleasant body odour, and this can cause difficulties with forming positive peer relationships. Girls can, on the surface, appear to be able to cope with the separation or divorce and therefore their reactions may not be displayed during their time in school but may materialise in the later teenage years and early adulthood and may then influence decisions and behaviour in their adult life. However, both boys and girls may:

  ▶ Equally be touched by nightmares, nail biting and speech difficulties.

  ▶ Present as anxious, jumpy, and restless and concentration may deteriorate.

  ▶ Become depressed.

  ▶ Be prone to infections, i.e. sore throats, ear infections and tummy upsets. This is particularly likely in the case of a bereavement, which follows an illness. The child may complain of symptoms similar to those of the dead person.

  ▶ Be reluctant to go to school.

  ▶ Become socially withdrawn.

  ▶ Become very anxious about being separated from parents.

  ▶ Bite nails or cuticles, pick/pull at themselves, twiddle with hair, rock or suck their thumb.

- Develop fears or phobias e.g. fear of the dark, fear of being left alone.

- Experience disturbed sleep. Some children have heard adult describe death as a kind of 'sleep' and they may consequently become afraid to sleep for fear that they may die.

- Have difficulty going to sleep and/or become lethargic.

- Have bad dreams or night terrors.

- Regress to an earlier stage of development i.e. using a 'baby' voice or 'losing' some previously gained skills.

- Start stammering or have other speech difficulties.

- Indulge more in daydreaming or fantasy escape.

- Show aggression.

- Be frightened to ask questions or talk, for fear of upsetting others. Some may only speak to certain significant adults or friends.

Whatever symptoms or behaviours are displayed, it is important that teachers in school can not only observe these but can also provide a safe and emotionally literate and secure environment in which children can journey through this process of grief and loss. This book will highlight some of the ways in which such a goal may be achieved whilst also supporting teachers and those working with children in schools. The aim is to develop our own awareness, knowledge, skills and insight into how we cope with death, loss and bereavement and how we can help support each other in this process.

Chapter Two

What Can Schools Do?

Understanding the process

Exploring and understanding the emotions involved in dealing with death and loss can be an area which schools and teachers are sometimes fearful of approaching because of its sensitive nature. This can also make it difficult to place on the curriculum. However, we would propose that fear should be left behind and that schools should and can embrace difficult subjects such as death, loss and bereavement. This can be used as a tool for developing not only the bereaved child's understanding of their loss but also other children's experience and understanding of death. Allowing the topic of death to be on the curriculum can facilitate children's understanding of the emotional journey and the feelings of loss and bereavement involved in this process. But most of all, it gives children a forum to develop their understanding and provides a platform for them to ask questions that they feel unable to ask those close to them who may also be bereaved. Mostly schools and teachers can help children develop a sense of the interrelating features in death, loss and bereavement, which brings together the whole person, the environment and the circumstances of bereavement. The role of the teacher is therefore to ensure that children are able to explore and discover the connections.

> 'Loss of a loved person is one of the most intensely painful experiences any human can suffer. And not only is it painful to experience but it is also painful to witness...To the bereaved nothing but the return of the lost person can bring true comfort.'
> Bowlby J (1988) *Loss, Sadness and Depression*

Children's experience of death or loss is something that many adults supporting them think that they will recover from very quickly after the event. It is thought that their grief will be short lived and will not impact on or affect their lives in any significant way. However, this perspective on children's experience of a death is not true. Children's expression of their feelings and their grief is different to adults to the extent that children may become quieter and less explicit in the way they manifest their emotions and communicate their thoughts. It is important that children are allowed and given the opportunity to overcome their grief. However, this is not always achieved because children are provided with less information than adults are. When there is a loss affecting the whole family it may be the case that the parents are not able to cope with their own grief, as well as their child's or children's grief. Additionally, some children are not provided with the possibility of exploring their loss, as adults believe that they should be protected from pain and therefore they are denied the chance to grieve. Consequently, they are not exposed to the same support systems as adults.

What do people need?

When coping with a death, people need the time and the space to grieve their loss and to learn to adjust their lives in order to accommodate this loss and cope with the death of a loved one. It is very difficult to say how much time should be allowed or given to a grieving individual. It is important to remember that the time people need will vary from situation to situation and will be dependent on factors such as the nature of the loss, the individual's age, their previous experiences, their personality and the support they are able to access. It has been suggested that grieving after a death can be a process that will last for up to two years. During this period, it is thought that the emotions of the bereaved are still unsettled and therefore a bereaved individual is unable to cope with emotionally challenging events and may not be able to support others' needs.

Grieving individuals will consequently need a familiar environment and people they can trust, as the absence of such factors can slow down the individual's ability to cope with their loss. It is also necessary to provide a safe comfort zone around bereaved individuals, and not to impose coping strategies on those who are suffering from a loss, ensuring that support is provided in a non-judgemental way, whereby individuals feel they are allowed to share their emotions without feeling criticised.

It is also important to remember that people are different and react differently to the stages of the grieving process. No one's grieving reactions are identical to another's. Nevertheless, it is acknowledged that disbelief, crying, anger and apathy are feelings that manifest themselves in all grieving processes.

The power and the importance of talking is a vital tool to help individuals develop and understand their loss. Using open-ended questions will encourage people to express their feelings. However, it is important that the communication of bereaved individuals is also linked to non-verbal communication and understanding and those working with bereaved people need to be aware of each individual's need for non-verbal communication and support.

Communication is an important vehicle in helping people deal with the pain of grief. Having the platform to talk and communicate their feelings whilst also maintaining the structures of familiar routines with the support and compassion of those around them is essential for 'good' grieving. It is also important for the bereaved to have opportunities to talk about how their feelings have changed as time goes by.

Most importantly, those working with or supporting bereaved children and adults need to be informed. This will help them understand and be able to adjust to the loss experience of others. Honesty is of great importance, as this will allow those who are grieving the chance to develop true perceptions and understandings of their situation.

It is very important to observe and understand how cultural and religious beliefs may also shape or influence the individual's reactions to death. It is important to understand that helping children to cope with death and coming to terms with their grief requires that they experience a secure relationship prior to their loss and are provided with open and honest information after the death, as well as given a forum in which they can have their questions answered. It is also vital for children to be active participants in rituals surrounding the death and to be offered the support and maintenance of a sustained relationship with a significant other. Adults and children need to proceed through the process of coping with death which involves four steps: accepting the reality of the loss, working through the pain of grief, adapting to life without the deceased and investing in new relationships. Such a process can be described as entirely cross-cultural.

Adapting to life without the deceased can be an enormous struggle and therefore it is important to keep the memory of the deceased alive. Additionally, it is beneficial to maintain contact with people who knew the deceased, as this can help to maintain a balanced view of the deceased's life. Keeping mementos and symbols to remember the deceased and marking important anniversaries is also a good idea. It is especially important to help the bereaved develop new interests and relationships without feeling that they are unable to reminisce about the past. They need to feel that they are being allowed to enjoy life and move on when they feel ready.

What can school staff offer children and colleagues?

As previously mentioned, school can be a constant feature in many children's lives whereas the events outside of the school context can appear to make life uncertain and insecure. The school can offer a valuable and consistent source of support as it plays such a significant part in children's lives.

'School makes up a large part of each day...Schools and teachers can make a difference to children who have experienced a bereavement and this can be a significant and important difference'. Wagner, P (1993)

Schools are diverse communities with a range of staff with many skills. The staff have different functions within the school, outside their main focus of teaching and learning. These various roles can focus on the pastoral side of children's education. School staff can consequently offer skills in listening to and communicating with children and other members of the school community. Listening and communicating can be the first stepping stones to building and facilitating the development of children's ability to address their issues of loss and the bereavement process as a whole.

In situations where schools have a child or children who are bereaved and are suffering from their loss, the best foundations are time, understanding and compassion to help children move towards accepting and overcoming their loss. Teachers need to highlight and reinforce the fact that this is a 'normal' process. As schools can be time conscious places, it is vital that time is the single component that is always given. This will allow the bereaved individual to feel less pressured.

Schools are familiar environments to children. They surround children with specific routines that can provide a secure environment, particularly for a bereaved child. The structure offered in a school may develop a sense of reality which reinforces the fact that life still goes on and that there are lots of possibilities for the future.

The support of friends and the school community is vital. At the outset, it is important that the bereaved child's peer group are made aware of the loss and given a opportunity to discuss feelings outside of the presence of the bereaved. Additionally, the bereaved child should be made aware of others' knowledge of their loss and their permission should be sought in advance of the disclosure, where possible. Mostly, bereaved children and their friends should be encouraged to re-establish their friendships and to talk together about the events that shape their lives.

School staff need to express their feelings and to show that they care about the child's loss. However, this should be done with a degree of emotional detachment, as coping with bereaved individuals can be emotionally challenging for all those concerned. The support that is offered to children by specialist 'outside' agencies or support staff as appropriate can always be extended to adults within the bereaved family.

Children spend a significant part of their day in school and with teaching staff. The relationship between a pupil and a teacher can engender a special bond of respect, nurture and caring. The role of the teacher in children's lives is consequently important and teachers and staff within the context of schools should not underestimate the significance of their roles. Teachers must understand and acknowledge that they can and do make a difference to children's lives, especially those who are emotionally challenged through experiencing a loss of a significant adult(s), as well as children who are living with adults who are equally challenged or learning to come to terms with changes in their own lives.

The role of teachers is not confined to the classroom context. It is both complex and diverse and dependent on the needs of individual pupils. When working with a bereaved child or children teachers need to establish a positive rapport through providing opportunities to listen and communicate in a truly authentic way. Consequently, it is very important that teachers understand both child development and the process of grief, in order to establish where the bereaved pupil is in terms of the mourning process.

Although schools are time pressured environments, it is generally the case that teachers can and do develop positive and authentic relationships with children. They will also ensure that sufficient time and space is allocated to those most in need.

Children going through the grief process require time to explore their feelings and to understand their world once again. Therefore, children within this position require the opportunity to gain positive affirmation and to learn that there is the possibility of succeeding despite their difficulties. This is clearly a central and important role for the teacher.

When taking on the role of the supporter in steering a child through the grief process, teachers need to promote the child's understanding that they are special and valued. It is important to convey that the loss is not fundamentally about rejection, as the value they have is based on their uniqueness and their worth to those around them. Developing a child's capacity to understand their uniqueness and value needs to be done sensitively. This will help them to take further steps in understanding their loss and grief. Essentially, the role of the supporter is to display and convey their concerns to the grieving individual(s) in a genuine and authentic way.

How can we support colleagues?

The processes involved in supporting individuals who are affected by loss and grief can be emotionally draining for those who are offering their support. It is consequently very important to ensure that support is offered to those supporting the bereaved.

This support can be provided in many ways and can take on many different forms. Essentially, support can be offered to staff and teachers who are providing support to the child through colleagues being aware of their role and understanding the stress that this may place upon them. Colleagues providing support may benefit from being offered personal and professional support, as their emotions may be challenged during the supporting process. They may well benefit from having opportunities to experience a calm and supportive atmosphere in which the resources they require are readily available. Most importantly, those working with bereaved individuals may need encouragement to seek specialist support as and when necessary.

Returning to school

One of the ways in which schools can support bereaved children is to encourage the return to school. There will be individual differences in terms of how much time a person may require, but it is important to understand that a long period of absence from school can cause difficulties. These difficulties may primarily occur in terms of readjustment, as the individual pupil will require support in addressing their anxieties around returning to school, as well as their separation anxiety which may manifest itself in not wanting to be separated from the remaining members of their family. Another area that will need to be addressed is helping the bereaved pupil to 'face' teachers and friends. The pupil will need support in discussing what the teachers and their friends know and learning how to cope with the ways in which teachers and their peers may treat them in relation to their experiences. Most importantly, a bereaved child will need to know about any individualised programme of support they can expect to receive and how this will be structured and provided.

Overall, it is vital to remember that a bereaved pupil will benefit from being treated with patience and understanding. The following strategies offer some basic guidance for staff who are attempting to facilitate the child's return to school:

▸ Give the pupil opportunities to talk about their feelings and ensure that time is allocated for this.

▸ Try and involve the bereaved pupil's close friends in the process, especially when encouraging the bereaved pupil to talk about their loss, in order to develop a situation where they can keep happy memories alive.

▸ Provide opportunities to answer the child's questions in a respectful and honest way.

▸ Encourage the pupil to explore his emotions and to understand and learn that their feelings are true and real and that they should not be ashamed to display them.

▸ It is important that adults working with pupils in the cycle of grieving for their loved one should refrain from saying, "You don't mean that, do you?" This will tend to diminish the child's responses and inhibit an authentic display of emotions and behaviours.

▸ It is also vital, wherever possible, that adults working with a bereaved child should help them to maintain contact and positive relationships with other family members/carers.

What can the school do to help?

The following suggestions may provide a helpful checklist for the member of staff with responsibility for coordinating the child's return to school.

▸ When a pupil returns to school after a bereavement, teachers and school staff should be informed about the pupil's situation. The pupil or pupils should be informed that staff are aware of their situation.

▸ The school and the pupil should together negotiate a contact person who should be available to the bereaved pupil or pupils when he needs to talk. This may be a member of the teaching staff or a member of the support staff who may well have developed a relationship with the child prior to his loss.

▸ When necessary (and dependent on the pupil's age), school should provide a suitable place for the pupil if she wants to take quiet 'time out' or needs some space to cope with the difficult emotions that they may be experiencing.

▸ Teachers and school staff should encourage the bereaved pupil's friends to offer him support and to provide a forum such as a 'Circle of Friends' in order to facilitate this support.

▸ Some children may benefit from being assigned an older pupil who can offer support when required. However, it is vital that this pupil also receives support in her role as a supporter to the bereaved child.

- Teachers and school staff should think about the needs of the whole family. It may be necessary to speak to them in order to gather information about what has happened and the importance or significance of any religious beliefs that they might hold.

- Teachers and school staff can help bereaved families by keeping them informed about how their child is coping in the school context.

- Teachers and school staff can also help bereaved families to understand that bereavement is a part of life and that its effects will be felt throughout life.

On-going observations

On-going observation of the pupil will allow teachers to ensure that the level and type of support remains appropriate. These observations involve learning to develop an understanding of the pupil, through understanding and taking cues from their behaviour. Consequently, it is important that staff working with bereaved children keep the following points in mind:

- Children's reactions to bereavement may differ. The emotional responses they may display include aggression, anger, fear, guilt and regression but no two individuals will respond in exactly the same way.

- The process of grieving can have negative effects on children's attainment and concentration. A bereaved child may need greater support in achieving and maintaining their concentration in and out of the classroom context.

- Self-identity is very important for any young person and it is very important that bereaved children have opportunities to re-establish their self-identity.

- Some children may not present grieving behaviour or may deny their grief. It is important to recognise this and to allow them the necessary space and time to go through the denial process and grieve in their own way.

- Teachers and school staff should help children understand that perceptions of death vary with age, and also that an individual's religious beliefs will play a major part in the grieving process.

- Teachers and school staff must be aware that children may seek out specific adults to speak to and therefore it is important that all members of staff involved are available to listen in an authentic way.

- It is usually helpful for adults working with a bereaved child to address their own feelings about death and bereavement.

- Adults should always provide a bereaved child with opportunities to have a quiet place to reflect. However, this needs to be done with sensitivity so that bereaved individuals are not be singled out visibly and offered special privileges which might make them stand out amongst their peers.

- Adults should help children become aware that death comes hand in hand with life and that it is a natural and necessary part of the life cycle.

- Teachers and school staff need to face up to the difficult topic of addressing issues of death on the school curriculum and relevant and appropriate information and materials on the topic of death should be available across all key stages.

- It is also vital to build up and maintain a positive home school link, as the types of support that can be offered to a bereaved family though having an open and supportive approach can be very difficult.

What can schools do through the taught curriculum?

Personal, Social and Health Education (PSHE) became a subject on the national curriculum in 1992 and schools have since had a legal obligation to ensure that all children benefit from a spiritual and moral curriculum. During the different key stages children are expected to understand the issues and rituals associated with birth, marriage and death. At Key Stage 1, children are expected to be able to discuss the emotions that take place at these significant periods of life. At Key Stage 2, pupils are expected to understand the process that is involved in death. This work is further extended in Key Stage 3 where children are asked to understand the nature of relationships in families when a death occurs. At Key Stage 4, pupils are expected to be aware of the impact of separation, loss and bereavement. Additionally, children at this stage should be able to know how to ask for support. Essentially, the nature of PSHE as a curriculum subject is, to some extent, dependent upon how a school wishes to interpret the curriculum and place emphasise on issues they deem to be of most importance. Occasionally, discussions on death may take a subordinate position in order that issues such as drugs and understanding relationships can be given a more a prominent role.

The role that teachers and school staff can play in helping children and young adults to understand and cope with the concept of death adds an important dimension to their work. The difficulties they face in doing this includes the problem of how to address the concept of death via the curriculum. However, we would argue that placing death, loss and bereavement on the curriculum can be done in a variety of ways, for example, through literature, plays and poems, as well as through role-plays and drama. Introducing the concept of death and loss can be done in a subtle way through curriculum areas such as English and Art through a process of exploring the experiences of others. In the science curriculum pupils can be given the opportunity to understand the life cycle of plants and animals. The history curriculum can shape children's view as to how death and life can take on a historical perspective. A major area of the curriculum which can provide an active forum for debate is, of course, the PSHE and Religious Education (RE) curriculum. These subjects particularly allow children to discuss their emotions and to consider ways of dealing with loss and death. This can be done via a range of activities and topics which particularly focus upon developing children's emotional literacy, self-awareness and problem-solving skills.

Topics which help to generate discussion and to promote children's understanding of loss, death and bereavement may include the following:

- ▸ feelings
- ▸ growing and changing
- ▸ moving house
- ▸ losing friends
- ▸ starting or changing schools
- ▸ new siblings
- ▸ adoption
- ▸ step-parents
- ▸ illness and being in hospital
- ▸ death and its rites and rituals.

The latter topic in the list highlights how different religious belief systems view life and also present the rituals involved in saying goodbye to the deceased. Not only can such a topic reinforce the universality of grief and loss but it can also aid the production of tolerance and understanding between different groups of children. The following summaries are intended as an aid to the teacher who wishes to discuss how the different belief systems celebrate and ritualise death and how they approach the grieving process. However, to really gain insight into each belief system it is probably most helpful to refer to appropriate literature and religious leaders or those who hold these particular beliefs.

Buddhist beliefs

The Buddhist faith states that everything in life is not permanent and that people are made up from separate elements. The physical form is seen to be linked to both sensations and perceptions. These elements disintegrate at death. Buddhists have a belief in Karma which represents the deeds or the actions of the individual. In Buddhist philosophy, an individual's previous actions will ensure that a new set of elements are reconstructed in order to create a new person. This belief system also includes the concept of Nirvana which is seen as permanent liberation from the cycle of life.

The Buddhist ceremony for the deceased will involve a coffin being decorated with flowers and gifts (normally given to the monks after the ceremony that is accompanied by prayers). The funeral will involve music and food, as Buddhists believe that death brings the deceased to Nirvana. Consequently, there is no display of grief or tears. For Buddhists the ideas encapsulated in the process of death focus on new life, calmness and acceptance. The body is cremated and a photograph is placed near the coffin as a symbol and reminder of the transient nature of life.

Christian beliefs

Christians believe in God and that Jesus is the Son of God. The Christian faith presents the concepts of heaven and hell and suggests that individuals can achieve eternal life. The view of death in the Christian faith is that death is a long sleep until all souls are resurrected.

The Christian approach to death and the manner in which the funeral is conducted is a means of affirming Christian belief and re-affirming faith in God. Burials or cremations are used to lay the body to rest. Grief is usually displayed with tears and this is sometimes encouraged as it is thought to help with the coping and grieving process.

Chinese Taoist beliefs

This view of life presents the twin forces of Yin and Yang which are thought to govern the universe. Life is seen as a balance between good and evil and the soul is divided into two parts. The higher spiritual soul with Yang is called Hun Soul and the other side of the soul is the P'O Soul (the earthly soul) with Yin. Taoists believe that when someone dies the soul takes on a spirit form and goes into the underworld. The P'O Soul is said to stay at the grave and should be fed to ensure that it doesn't turn into a wicked ghost. The idea of heaven is also encompassed and this is seen as a place where ancestors live. They are described as controlling earthly things. Taoist beliefs state that the deceased will become ghosts and after three years each ghost must be honoured. This faith purports that heaven can be achieved by passing through 'courts'.

The funeral rituals are based on the philosophy that death is not the end but a passage to move onto a new unconnected sphere focusing on spiritual wellbeing. The funeral ritual is thought to help the Hun Soul onto its underworld journey. The colour for mourning is white and drums, cymbals, fireworks and music are used to scare the evil sprits away. The deceased are burned and paper models of cars, houses and money are also burnt as a means of helping the dead through the after life. After ten years the coffin is dug up and Feng Shui (divination) is used by the priest in order to find the right place for the deceased to be re-buried. Each year there is a festival called Ching-Ming, which celebrates and remember the dead.

Humanist beliefs

Humanists believe that death is a natural ending to life and that there is no after life or heaven. Most humanists believe that there is no supernatural dimension. The funeral practices in the Humanist tradition suggest that there is no need for a ceremony. However, usually a non religious funeral takes place. This ceremony is done in accordance with the family's wishes. The ceremony would usually be a celebration and commemoration of the life of the deceased.

Hindu beliefs

The Hindu faith proposes that each person has a soul that is both permanent and unchanging. According to this faith, when someone dies the soul loses its human body and puts on another body which may not be human. This shedding and changing of the soul will continue a cycle of re-births until the soul reaches God. Hinduism states that during life a person passes through sixteen stages called Samskaras. The physical body is thought to be made up of fire, air, earth and water. Hindus view cremation as bringing the physical body back to fire and air, while burial of the physical body returns it back to the earth.

During Hindu funeral ceremonies the deceased is normally cremated within 24 hours of their death. The coffin is covered with flowers prior to the cremation. Readings concerning reincarnation are read from the holy books. After three days the ashes are cooled and scattered on a river (Ganges when possible). The role of friends and family is vital as they bring gifts to the bereaved relatives. On the eleventh to the thirteenth day all involved will gather together to offer Pinda (rice and milk) to the deceased person, and thanks for the good things in life. In a family where there is an eldest son or male relative he will shave his head as a sign of bereavement. After the thirteenth day, public mourning ceases and there is a large feast. The memory of the deceased is then manifested through daily worship (Puja).

Islamic beliefs

Muslims believe that there is one God called Allah and the prophet of God is called Mohammed. Muslims believe that there is only one life and that there will be a judgement day in which each soul will be judged according to their deeds and actions whilst alive. This faith suggests that when a person dies their soul is looked after by the angel of death until judgement is passed. If the grief displayed is too bold and extravagant this can be perceived as being rebellion against the will of Allah.

Burial takes place within 24 hours of the death. Mourning is demonstrated through reading the Qur'an and coffins are not used unless law stipulates it. The body is normally washed, perfumed and wrapped in three pieces of white cotton called a 'shroud'. The body will then be buried face downwards towards Makkkah. A traditional ceremony requires that the families stay at home for three days after the funeral. The grave should be visited every Friday for forty days. The mourning period will last up to three months and usually during this period there will be no celebrations or weddings.

Jewish beliefs

The Jewish belief system proposes that there is one God and there is only one life to be lived. There is a belief in heaven and hell and the ways in which these places should focus individuals on trying to be faithful to God in their lives. Orthodox Jews believe in the resurrection of the body and therefore cremation is forbidden. However, reformed Jews believe in 'life eternal' and the resurrection of the body. Orthodox Jews also believe in the coming of a Messiah in which all souls will return to their bodies.

In this belief system the body should be buried with 24 hours. The body is cleaned, dressed and placed in a plain coffin. The coffin is usually taken to the synagogue and then to the cemetery where each of the closest male relatives will say a prayer (Kaddish) and everyone will help fill the grave with earth. After the funeral, the family will mourn for a whole week and friends will provide food and encourage the bereaved to express their grief. The bereaved family will not participate in any celebrations during their mourning. For a period of up to eleven months prayers (Kaddish) are said every day. A longer period is required for those individuals who were considered to be 'wicked'. Each year families will mark the anniversary of a death when they will say Kaddish and burn a candle for 24 hours. Visiting the grave should be done at least once a year, so as to ensure the memories do not fade, as well as to comfort the bereaved.

Sikh beliefs

The Sikh faith advocates that there is one God. It identifies both a heaven and a hell. However, these places are seen as temporary places for the soul until it returns to the earth, after resting. There will be a union with God after death and this is described as 'merging' with God. Sikhism does not encourage mourning as this is thought to symbolise a desire to keep separate from God. Death is welcomed in this religion as it is seen as bringing the deceased closer to God.

The Sikh funeral process involves friends and relatives saying Sukhmans which are psalms and songs of peace from the holy book (Guru Granth Sahib). The coffin is taken to the Gurdwara where ceremonies take place. Cremation is the norm and the male relatives normally attend this. After the cremation, the focus is given to back to the Gurdwara where readings, prayers and hymns are said. This is followed by the distribution of Kara Parshad and a large feast. The funeral ceremony ends with a feast as this symbolises that life continues. The ashes of the deceased are scattered into a holy river. The mourning process involves a period of ten days where the family will read from the Guru Granth Sahib.

What should a policy address?

Schools need to take on an active role in introducing the ideas of loss, death and bereavement to the curriculum. It is consequently vital to develop a whole-school policy which identifies the rationale for the introduction of loss, change, death and bereavement. This process should be consultative and should draw from the ideas of all staff. The curriculum must cater for each phase of education. It must also be a working document and should be reviewed and developed on an on-going basis and in the light of the events which shape both the children's and staff's lives.

The curriculum should consequently encourage participants to explore and draw upon their own experiences.

It should also be able to address children's questions and concerns. These questions and concerns should be accompanied with opportunities to learn about customs, rituals and practices associated with death and dying. The policy should be explicit about how children, adults, parents and carers are supported during and after such a loss and the specific process involved in supporting the individual child back into the school community.

How can schools help parents or carers?

Teachers and school staff need to recognise that families, parents and carers will need support when dealing with a loss or suffering from a bereavement. During these difficult times parents are sometimes unaware of whom to turn to for support. There are many different ways in which teachers and school staff can support parents. These include the following:

- By helping parents to actualise their loss through encouraging them to talk about events.

- By understanding that parents may benefit from being encouraged to understand and express their views and feelings. These may include anger, fear, crying alongside feelings of guilt and blame. Parents with these feeling will need to develop an understanding that their feelings are normal and part of the cycle of grieving. One thing parents must be assured of is the fact that just because they are having difficulties coping with their grief and they feel that they are consequently not supporting their child this does not mean that they love their child less.

- By keeping parents fully informed about the needs of their child as they will benefit from knowing how the school is supporting her. This information may also help them further support their child in the home context.

- By ensuring that they are encouraged to acknowledge that time is very important and that time to adjust is essential. Also, that every individual is unique and will require different amounts of time and utilise different strategies in coming to terms with their feeling of loss.

- By providing parents with access to other 'outside' agencies who can help them to accept the reality of their situation and to develop ways of moving on in order to create and construct a positive future.

- By helping parents establish good networks for communication with other professionals, so that parents are not burdened by a number of professionals at any one time i.e. avoiding support or professional overload.

- By avoiding the use of jargon when communicating with parents. Clear communication is so important as it will impact upon their understanding and reduce further anxiety.

- By taking the initiative in offering support to parents. Parents may be afraid to seek help or advice because of fear that they are wasting time or because they are afraid that school staff feel that they are unable to cope.

- By helping parents to notice their strengths and further support them by providing on-going positive feedback on the way in which they are supporting their child/children within the home context.

Chapter Three

Working with the Individual Child

What is best practice?

This chapter is designed to help those working with individual children and young adults suffering from a loss/bereavement. Essentially, the best help adults can offer children is to be available and authentic in their emotional responses and interactions. The following suggestions are not intended as a straitjacket or a list of 'must do's'. They are intended to provide practical advice and strategies as to the most appropriate ways to support the bereaved child. So, when a death occurs and a child is bereaved we would ask the teachers/adults involved to attempt the following (as appropriate and when feasible):

Providing protection

During times of change and loss many children will need to feel that they have both support and companionship. They will benefit from being shielded from the many pressures they may experience, including sudden changes or new demands. This protection comes in the form of allowing them to deal with their emotions in a protected environment with the support of the peer group. It is very important to remember that some children may feel more comfortable expressing their emotions with their peers and normally having a best friend/buddy at school can help the bereaved child with any difficulties they may encounter in the playground and with school staff.

Empathy

When helping children and young adults cope with their loss it is important for staff and peers to develop a sense of empathy i.e. to see the world through the bereaved child or children's eyes. At times, adults may recognise the anxieties a child or children may have and conclude that these fears are unfounded. It is extremely important for adults to convey to the child that their fears are unfounded and this should be done in a sensitive way that ensures that the bereaved child does not feel ridiculed.

Showing unconditional regard

Children coping with the process of grieving will need to feel that those around them care for them, regardless of the things they do. Therefore, it is important that teachers and staff working with a bereaved child put aside their own personal feelings towards them and show them positive regard. They need to avoid being judgemental in any way as children will cope better in environments which they find supportive and where they are free of fear of reprimand or ridicule. Any feelings of condemnation or disapproval should not cloud the support provided, as children suffering from bereavement may feel out of their depth and any additional pressure simply causes further distress.

Ensuring confidentiality and trust

The relationship that is established between the supporting adult and the grieving child requires the adult to be open in terms of exhibiting a balanced and compassionate stance in which the child's perspective is accepted no matter how difficult this process becomes. The supporting adult must also be aware that they may become the object of hostility as well as a source of support. The relationship between the two parties can be both a strained and fulfilling one. However, the bond that develops should be based on the underlying principles of confidentiality and truth. The issue of confidentiality must clearly be shaped by the school's regulations and the Local Education Authority's (LEA) policy. Teachers and school staff should not place themselves in a position where they promise to keep something secret and know that it is unfeasible to do so because the information they receive may place the child at risk in some way.

Along with the issue of confidentiality, it is important for children to be able to trust the adults working with them. Adults must be made aware that lying to any child can cause many difficulties, especially if the child later finds out the truth. When this happens, children find it impossible to trust in the future. By the same token, it is important that teachers and school staff do not make promises that they cannot keep.

Avoiding the dependency cycle

Learning to cope with a loss can place a child in a different role in which he becomes more dependent upon the adults around them. As the child moves through a sea of emotions he may tend to warm towards an adult who appears to totally understand their needs. Teachers and school staff need to be careful that they do not encourage a dependency cycle, where the child feels that the adult is the only person who will be able to support him. A bereaved child will need a balance. He should have someone to turn to when he wants to share his concerns, but should also be encouraged and helped to simultaneously develop his independence and self-confidence. Helping children to feel positive about themselves will further foster their belief and confidence both in others and themselves. They will also be able to further develop a sense of self-worth.

Knowing when to move on

Sometimes a child can become stuck in their grief. It can consequently be helpful to encourage the bereaved child to look closely at the world around her, especially the natural world. Reminding a grieving child of 'small deaths' that occur in the natural world everyday is useful here but it is important not to trivialise her feelings. The bereaved child needs to understand that death is the ultimate separation and that it is absolutely natural she will feel pain as she comes to terms with her situation. Such 'pain' is felt, to different degrees, by those suffering both 'small' and 'big' deaths.

It is important to recognise that some children may need further support in coping with their bereavement, especially when there is a traumatic circumstance surrounding the death. Children who are 'stuck' in their grief may manifest certain behaviours, as their devastation is simply too much for them to bear. These manifestations may take the following forms:

- ▶ Anti-social behaviour such as stealing and damage to property.
- ▶ Anxious, compulsive care giving.
- ▶ Being accident-prone.
- ▶ Death fears – the child experiences continued anxiety about her own death, despite reassurances.
- ▶ Denial – the child cannot accept that their parents will not get back together or that their dead relative will not come back home again.
- ▶ Destructive behaviour, including self-harm.
- ▶ Failure to thrive, failure to gain the appropriate height and weight for his age.
- ▶ Inability to successfully play or mix with peer group.
- ▶ Loss of hope – the child is listless and gains little pleasure from food, friendship or activities.

- Regression – school performance and behaviour seems frozen or regresses to an earlier developmental stage and shows no sign of change.

- School phobia.

School staff, parents and carers will need to carefully analyse such behaviours in order to make a decision regarding the need for further specialist therapeutic support such as counselling from a Mental Health Service.

Adhering to your 'Golden Rules'

It is always difficult to know how to help a child deal with their loss. Many teachers, mentors and carers are concerned about what they can do and say to a grieving child in order to help. We have formulated a list of 'Golden Rules' which we have found to be helpful to adults and other children in supporting children in both expressing their grief and in dealing with the pain of loss. These are as follows:

- Accept that the bereaved child's feeling might be very different to yours.

- Be there 'in the silence' too: some children don't want to talk.

- Be there to listen if the child wants to talk.

- Be truthful and answer questions honestly.

- Empathise and try not to say 'I know exactly what you feel'.

- Encourage the child to express emotions rather than keeping them bottled up.

- Give the child time to grieve, there is nothing to be gained by rushing it.

- If you are too upset to help, find a friend or relative to stand in for you for a while.

- Involve the child in practical tasks and decisions both in and out of the school context.

- As far as possible, it is a good idea to keep to familiar surroundings and predictable routines.

- Show the child love, care and consistency as these will act as healing tools.

- Reassure the child that strong feelings are a normal part of grieving.

- Remember to share positive and happy memories and have a laugh. Ask the child about the happy times and good memories that they have.

- Show you care by giving the time the child needs.

- Ensure that the child understands that the pain of loss is a part of life – it is not something to be ashamed of.

- Remember that the parents of a child who has experienced loss may be so caught up in their own loss that they may not notice what is happening to their child. You may be the most stable, consistent influence in his life.

- Acknowledge the fact that a bereaved child may feel very different from his peers.

- If the child exhibits aggressive behaviour then talk to them about the outcome of their actions and give them the freedom to choose how to deal with it. This overcomes the feeling of helplessness and emphasises the feeling of being in control.

- Be sensitive to delayed grief responses and remember that there is no single time scale for coming to terms with loss.

- Always seek clarification if you don't understand something, or feel you have missed a point. Clear it up by asking a relevant question.

- It maybe helpful to compile a book of tributes, letters, poems and pictures from classmates and staff members.

- Discreetly praise pupils who make the effort to support a child who has experienced loss; they are using important social skills that will help them throughout life.

- Encourage pupils to seek support from friends and family whenever they need it. They will tend to 'know' what is appropriate for them at the time and tend to seek out the most relevant person.

- Sometimes extra layers of clothing can help a child feel especially cared for and layered against the possibility of harm.

- If a pupil has died it is sometimes preferable to leave a gap where their workspace was and to work around it. It gives the children permission to grieve. Gradually the space will be filled when the time is right.

- It is helpful to keep a hot water bottle as a comforter for younger children, as some children who suffer loss may feel cold from the shock. As well as warming them, a hot water bottle will give them something to hold on to.

▸ Ensure that the children have opportunities to regularly work in pairs or small groups. When the upset pupil cannot concentrate the others will help him carry on.

▸ Always remember to listen for feelings – don't just concentrate on the facts as these are often less important than the feelings. Also, listen for overtones – you can learn a great deal from the way the person says things and what they do not say.

▸ If it is appropriate, mark critical events with an act such as planting a tree, dedicating a trophy or a book to the deceased person.

▸ Ensure that you provide creative outlets for hurt in painting, writing and drama.

▸ Remember to speak to the pupil using age appropriate language but without being patronising.

▸ When talking with the child, periodically check back that you have heard them correctly by summarising the main points of what has been said. You may wish to encourage them to do the summary.

▸ Always talk positively about the deceased person without making them into a saint.

▸ The best way to deal with the physical release of anger is to respect the energy zone and devise a permitted expression for feelings. For example, 'When you have that hitting feeling, you may not hit Daniel but you may hit your pillow or bang your fists on the table,' or 'What you are doing is not safe for you. I want you to take care of yourself.' This approach avoids the conflict that will occur if the child is told, 'Don't do that.' Suggested materials to have on hand to use as a means for release of anger are – newsprint, clay, reinforced cardboard blocks, foam bats, punching bags, inflated clowns, jointed play people and animals, hammer and nails.

▸ Use music to help distressed pupils to relax if they seem to respond positively to such a resource.

▸ Where a child has been off school for some time, always try to visit the home and talk about what it will be like to return to school. It is essential to plan for this event.

▸ For children a funeral can be a frightening situation, where the displays of emotions can be overwhelming. Many children are not totally aware of what takes place at a funeral and therefore they create fantasies about funerals and cremations. It is important that adults supporting a bereaved child talk about what they will likely experience and see at a funeral or a cremation.

▸ Children can be afraid that they will lose their memory of their loved one and having a memory box can provide the link between the future, present and the past. Help the child to set up their own Memory Box.

▸ Use Memory Stones to offer the bereaved child an opportunity to reminisce. Rocky stones can symbolise the memories that still hurt and have sharp edges. Smooth stones can represent the neutral memories, and special memories can be represented by polished gemstones – golden memories!

Chapter Four

Portraits, Poems and Pictures

Notes for teachers, mentors and carers

The following 35 worksheets are designed to be used mainly on an individual basis with young children who are in the process of coping with the feelings of loss and separation associated with the death of a loved one. They are not intended to provide a structured course of treatment or therapy, but rather to encourage the child to understand the effects of loss – physical, mental and emotional and to accept that they have a right to mourn and to expect others to support them in the process.

Consequently, the worksheets aim to address some of the fears, emotions and conflicting thoughts and resulting behaviours that the child may be experiencing. Areas covered are as follows:

▸ Identifying those you can talk to and who can help you in the grieving process.

▸ Identifying and articulating current feelings and needs alongside future goals and wishes.

▸ The importance of saying goodbye.

▸ How and when we can talk about those we have lost and the need to take time to do so.

▸ How time can change and affect our feelings, responses and behaviours.

▸ The value and importance of memories and the need to collect and treasure these.

- Rituals and rites surrounding death and how these help us to cope with our losses.

- The permanence of death and the fact we cannot 'bring the person back' to our world.

- How poems, pictures and portraits can help us to identify our feelings and help us to cope.

- Encouraging the child to talk about their dreams to identify who can help them to cope when they experience frightening or sad dreams.

- The importance of identifying and holding onto positive experiences and qualities of the person we have lost whilst also acknowledging and accepting those faults or foibles which were also a part of them.

- Acknowledging the existence of a life cycle and the fact that death is a process common to all living things as are birth, change and loss.

- The value and importance of visiting the place of burial and commemorating the death and life of a loved one.

- Accepting that angry feelings may result from loss and knowing that it is OK and often very important to acknowledge and articulate these feelings.

- The importance of crying and showing grief with others who are also bereaved.

- Coping with feelings of loneliness and the ways in which we may experience these in various ways and at various times.

- Acknowledging and understanding the wide range of often disturbing and conflicting feelings (for example, guilt, relief and fears) that we may experience in this process.

- Understanding and identifying how friends can help us through the process.

- The importance of observing and empathising with others who are also experiencing loss.

- The importance of understanding how our lives will continue and that we will experience happiness and do not need to feel guilty about having positive experiences – even in the face of our losses.

- How we need to balance solitary grieving with showed grieving in order not to become 'stuck'.

- Identifying and clarifying useful self-help or stress-management strategies and approaches.

> ▸ Helping the child to create a personalised memory booklet or series of memory objects, e.g. a stone or special box, to support the grieving process.

Using the worksheets

There is no particular order for making use of these worksheets just as there is no 'right' way of presenting the sheets to the individual child. The sheets may be used in a one to one therapeutic context, within a nurture group, with special friends/carers or independently. It is hoped that the teacher, parent, carer or mentor will be able to judge not only the most appropriate sequence but also the most fitting and sensitive way of using these frameworks with each individual child.

The worksheets can be used as part of the process of adapting to life without the deceased and the investing in and building of new relationships. This process will clearly be a part of the school and home support systems which will need to be put in place for the child at this time.

The sheets can provide frameworks for 'Talk Times' which may be allocated curriculum time provided on an individual needs and requirement basis. They may also form a significant part of a child's attempts to construct a 'Memory Book' or 'Special Book of remembrance'.

There should be no pressure placed upon the child to fully complete the sheets. It may also be appropriate to simply use the frameworks as prompts for the discussion time or for the teacher, parent, carer or mentor to simply record the child's thoughts on the sheets. What is important is that the child feels able to set his own agenda and to utilise any 'talk time' to discuss individual concerns, feelings and problems. The worksheets can be used to 'fit in' with this process. For example, if a child is experiencing some 'bad' dreams and finding these difficult to cope with it may be helpful to make use of the 'Dreams' worksheet to record or discuss these. If a child feels that it is his fault that someone has died this could be addressed through the 'It's not your fault!' worksheet. The on-going observations of the adult will be crucial in terms of determining how and when the sheets are used. Key to this process is the need for the adult to continually listen, observe and to be sensitive and afford respect to the individual child.

The following list details the nature and content of each of the 35 worksheets and provides some indicator as to when it may be appropriate or useful to make use of each sheet.

The worksheets

▸ **Worksheet 1 Scaling Activity** – this solution focused process can help the child to consider their present state and to identify how they can move forwards in a positive way and also who can help them in this process.

▸ **Worksheet 2 Saying Goodbye** – to help the child to identify and label the many feelings they will experience in this process and to help them to understand that all their feelings are valid and that nobody has the right to judge them for having any particular feeling.

▸ **Worksheet 3 Talking Through Time** – to help the child to begin to talk about their loved one. To ensure the child knows that it is OK to wait to talk and that views and feelings may well change over time.

▸ **Worksheet 4 My Memory Book** – to encourage the child to make a 'Memory Book' and to identify a list of things that might be included in such a document.

▸ **Worksheet 5 My Special Person** – to show the child that it can help to remember a special person through photos, pictures and drawings. It is important to remember how special they were to us.

▸ **Worksheet 6 Farewell Messages** – to help the child prepare for a funeral by encouraging some discussion about the burial process and the rituals that accompany it.

▸ **Worksheet 7 Magic Moments** – to help the child understand the permanence of death i.e. we cannot 'magic' the person back to life. What we can do is remember and celebrate all the special 'magic moments' that we shared with them.

▸ **Worksheet 8 Letters** – this can help the child who feels that he very much want to talks to the deceased person in order to convey how he feels and how he felt about them.

▸ **Worksheet 9 Dreams** – this sheet can be used to help the child who is experiencing 'sad' or 'bad' dreams to begin to describe these and to identity those who may be able to support her in this coping process.

▸ **Activity 10 Best Bits** – to help the child remember and celebrate the best qualities of the deceased.

▸ **Activity 11 New Life** – to encourage the child to see death as one part of the life cycle and to begin to accept that new life will follow and this needs to be valued and appreciated as much as the old life.

▸ **Activity 12 Visiting and Remembering** – this sheet may be used to help the child prior/after a visit to the place of burial. He may experience a range of sometimes conflicting feelings and memories at such a time and it is important to provide a forum in which these can be validated and discussed further.

▸ **Worksheet 13 Things I Loved About You** – another opportunity to remember and articulate the special and loveable qualities of the deceased which are entirely personal to the individual child.

▸ **Worksheet 14 Angry Feelings** – to help the child who experiences anger at the loss of their loved one and to assure them that this is acceptable and entirely normal. This can act as a prompt to considering the best ways to show and manage such strong feelings.

▸ **Worksheet 15 Feeling Loved** – to help the child to identify how love is expressed and the fact that it can be unconditional i.e. it doesn't matter how naughty or 'bad' I was _____ still loved me and showed me that this was the case. You should be sensitive about giving this sheet to looked after children as it's not appropriate for many of them.

▸ **Worksheet 16 Crying** – to help the child understand that this is an entirely normal and healthy process. It is important to express sadness in this way rather than 'bottle it up'. We can also share this process with others and know that crying can be both a solitary and a shared experience.

▸ **Worksheet 17 Time to Talk** – helps the child understand how important it is to make time to talk about the person that we loved. It may also be possible, and indeed necessary, to identify all those with whom she can talk in this way.

▸ **Worksheet 18 Draw the Anger** – this sheet can be used as a follow on activity to sheet 14. 'Drawing Anger' is a way of coping with this feeling and expressing it in a safe way. This sheet provides a prompt to considering other anger management strategies or ways of expressing themselves and which may be personal to the individual child.

▸ **Worksheet 19 Lonely Lorna** – this sheet may be used to prompt the development of empathy. Also, if a child is withdrawing or feeling particularly lonely it may enable him to identify a way forward without actually having to identify himself as the 'lonely' person.

▸ **Worksheet 20 Rainy Days** – considering how the environment can cause us to feel happy or sad and to recall either positive or negative times and memories.

▸ **Worksheet 21 Too Many Feelings** – this sheet could be used to help the child identify and articulate the wide range of feelings that she may be experiencing and to begin to understand that this is entirely normal.

- **Worksheet 22 Perfect Portrait** – using drawing as a tool for remembering and celebrating the deceased and loved one.

- **Worksheet 23 Fabulous Friends** – to encourage the child to identify the ways in which their friends may be able to help them through the bereavement process. This worksheet encourages them to be specific about how they would like their friends to behave and respond to them and consequently can help the teacher, parent, carer or mentor to maintain an appropriately supportive social context.

- **Worksheet 24 It's Not Your Fault!** – this sheet can be used with the child who presents as blaming themselves in some way for the death of the loved one or special person. The problem-solving task depersonalises the situation and may subsequently act as a prompt to further discussion of the child's own feelings.

- **Worksheet 25 Good and Bad Memories** – not all memories will be good, as no person and no situation are perfect. It is important not to feel guilty for acknowledging the negatives and to identify ways of coping with bad memories.

- **Worksheet 26 Look and Listen** – encouraging the child to consider others who may be grieving and to identify how they might be supportive and show empathy for them.

- **Worksheet 27 Remembering a Loved One** – focusing on how we can celebrate someone's life through special events and celebrations and that these occasions can be joyful and fun as well as being sad and serious.

- **Worksheet 28 It's Okay to be Happy** – helping the child to acknowledge that she can and will be happy in the future. Also, to understand that it is OK to be happy now – even in the grieving process there will be moments of happiness and we should accept and value these rather than feel guilty about having them.

- **Worksheet 29 Leave Me Alone!** – sometimes we need to take time out to grieve for a loved one but it is important to strike the right balance between solitary mourning and the sharing of grief and sadness. This worksheet may be useful for the child who is finding the sharing process difficult.

- **Worksheet 30 New Life** – to help the child see death as part of the life cycle and to recognise how new life and growth can help the healing process.

- **Worksheet 31 Reaching Out** – another reinforcement of the need to share our grief and to reach out to others in the process. It is important that the child can identify and understand the variety of ways of showing grief/reaching out to others i.e. we don't just have to talk!

- ▸ **Worksheet 32 Look After Yourself - Stress Busters** – a useful sheet for helping the child to identify and make use of a range of stress management strategies. It is helpful to acknowledge the fact that stress is person specific and that what works for her may not be as effective a strategy for others and vice versa.

- ▸ **Worksheet 33 Peaceful Places** – a useful relaxation strategy which can help the child to find moments of peace and escape from the stresses of the grieving process.

- ▸ **Worksheet 34 Write About It** – for the child who likes to express his feelings in writing, this can be a useful strategy and may prompt the child to maintain a diary during these times.

- ▸ **Worksheet 35 Scaling Activity 2** – this solution-focused process may be used with the child after a few months or even one or two years after the initial bereavement. Again, as with the earlier Scaling Activity, it can help the child consider their present state and to identify how they can move forward in a positive way and those who can help them through such a process.

Scaling Activity

Colour the leaf that shows where you are now on the scale of 1 -10.

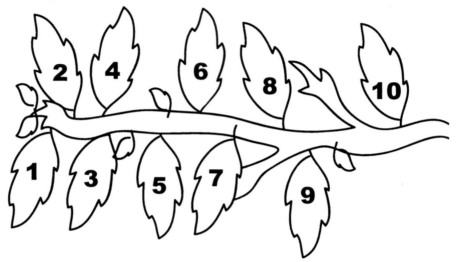

Now answer these questions:

Where am I now?

_____

Why have I rated myself as…?

_____

Where would I like to be?

_____

How can I get there? What do my targets need to be?

_____

Who else can help me?

_____

How will I know when I've reached my goal? What will I feel like and what will be happening?

_____

Saying Goodbye

Saying goodbye to someone we love is not always easy. It can cause us to feel upset, sad or even relieved or guilty.

Think about the feelings that you have experienced.

Can you use these to complete an acrostic poem?

S _____

A _____

Y _____

I _____

N _____

G _____

G _____

O _____

O _____

D _____

B _____

Y _____

E _____

Talking Through Time

Sometimes we can talk about a special person immediately after they have died.
Sometimes we need to wait for a short time and sometimes for quite a while.

Some questions to think about:

1. What would you say about your special person at this time?

_____

_____

2. Do you think that you might say something else or something different next month?

_____

_____

3. What do you think you will say and feel this time next year?

_____

_____

4. Do you think that time passing will help you? If so, how and why?

_____

_____

My Memory Book

Sometimes it is helpful to make a memory book in order to remember a special person. This can include all sorts of things such as your favourite photos, poems, pictures or mementos. What would you include in your book? Make a list.

A list of things to go in my Memory Book:

My Special Person

Draw a picture of something that reminds you of your special person. Sometimes it can help to remember special items such as a football, a book, a pair of glasses or a favourite scarf.

Farewell Messages

Sometimes when people die, they are placed in coffins which are then buried near to a holy place, or another special place of burial. Sometimes we put flowers on the grave and the dead person's family will put a special headstone over the grave to show where they are buried. Sometimes they will write or engrave a message on the stone.

What would you say in your message?

_____

_____

_____

_____

_____

_____

_____

Magic Moments

Sometimes we wish that we could 'magic' our special people back when they have died. We can't do this but we can remember all those 'magic moments' that we had with them. Can you remember some of yours? Write or draw about them in the stars.

Letters

Write a note to your special person and tell them how you feel.

Address ....

....

....

Date ....

Dear

....

....

....

....

....

....

....

....

Love

Dreams

When someone dies they are not asleep although it may look that way at first. When we go to sleep we may often dream about that special person. Some of these dreams will be happy while others may be sad or even frightening. Can you remember some of your dreams?

Happy Dreams   Sad Dreams

_____   _____

_____   _____

_____   _____

_____   _____

Who can help you if you have a sad dream? Can you explain what help you need?

Best Bits

Write about your special person's best qualities in the thought bubbles.

New Life

The Qur'an says 'Every soul shall have a taste of death'. (21,35) Although this seems sad we need to remember that this is just one part of the life cycle. As one plant dies, another begins to grow and flower. Can you design a beautiful plant or flower in honour of your special person?

Visiting and Remembering

When we visit a place of burial we can experience lots of different things.

List some of your memories and feelings.

Memories

Feelings

Things I Loved About You

Draw these inside the frame.

Angry Feelings

When someone dies we can feel very angry. This is normal and we shouldn't be scared of showing these feelings. Sometimes we are angry that they have gone away and left us and sometimes we are angry with ourselves for some of the things we did or didn't do when they were alive.

Can you record your angry thoughts and feelings in the speech bubbles? Who can talk to you about these? Who can help you deal with them?

Feeling Loved

When people love you they will look after you even if you are naughty or do something wrong.

Draw a picture of your special person showing how and why they made you feel loved.

Crying

Crying is one way to show that we are feeling sad and to express that sadness. Sometimes we need to cry alone. Sometimes it is good to cry with others and share our tears. Can you draw the people that you cry with? Use the mini-portrait frames and label your pictures.

Time to Talk

We need to talk about special people in our lives and to say how we felt about them when they were alive and how we feel about them now that they are dead. We sometimes need to make 'time to talk'.

When can you talk about your special person? Who can you talk to?

Write your ideas in the speech bubbles.

Draw the Anger

What does anger look like? When you feel angry what kind of things would you draw in order to show it? Have a go at drawing your anger in this frame.

How do you feel once you have done this? Can you think of other ways of safely showing your anger?

Lonely Lorna

Lorna is feeling very lonely because her best friend has died. She is quite shy and finds it difficult to make new friends. She is also very sad and misses her friend a lot. Can you think of ways that you and your friends could help her? Write a list of ideas.

Lorna's List
We could help Lorna by:

_____

_____

_____

_____

_____

_____

_____

_____

Rainy Days

Draw how you might feel on a rainy day. Sometimes you might feel sad and miss your special person more. If you sit in front of a warm fire and think about some of the happy memories you might feel less sad. Think and reflect – then make your picture below.

Too Many Feelings

When someone dies we think and feel lots of different things. Put a tick next to those feelings on the list that you have felt or feel now.
Can you add any more to the list?

☐ Lost   ☐ Cold

☐ Angry   ☐ Guilty

☐ Worried   ☐ Confused

☐ Afraid   ☐ It's my fault

☐ Tired   ☐ Hurt

☐ Stunned   ☐ Muddled

☐ Sad   ☐ Fed-up

☐ Lonely   ☐ _____

☐ _____ ☐ _____

☐ _____ ☐ _____

☐ _____ ☐ _____

☐ _____ ☐ _____

Perfect Portrait

Can you draw a portrait of the person you loved?
Use the frame below.

Fabulous Friends

When we are feeling sad and lonely, and missing the people that we love, our friends can often help us. Imagine that you have a special friend. What would you like this person to do and say and how would you like them to act around you? Record you ideas in the shapes below.

It's Not Your Fault!

Gemma is feeling very guilty and sad. She had an argument with her dad because he would not give the money for some new clothes and trainers. She got angry with him and said he was really mean and that she hoped he'd die because if it were just her and her mum then she would have been allowed to have the money. Gemma's dad died of cancer eight months later. Now she feels that it was her fault and can't stop crying and thinking about the horrible thing she said to her dad. What would you suggest can help her? Can you write a note to Gemma and explain to her that it is not her fault?

Dear Gemma

_____

_____

_____

_____

_____

_____

_____

_____

From

_____

Good and Bad Memories

Draw and label your good and bad memories in the two columns:

Good	Bad

How can you cope with these memories?

_____

_____

_____

Who can help you?

_____

_____

Look and Listen

When someone in the family dies lots of people will be feeling sad and very upset. It is important for everyone to look out for each other and listen to what everyone has to say.
Who can you look out for?
Draw them or write a message to each on in the frames.

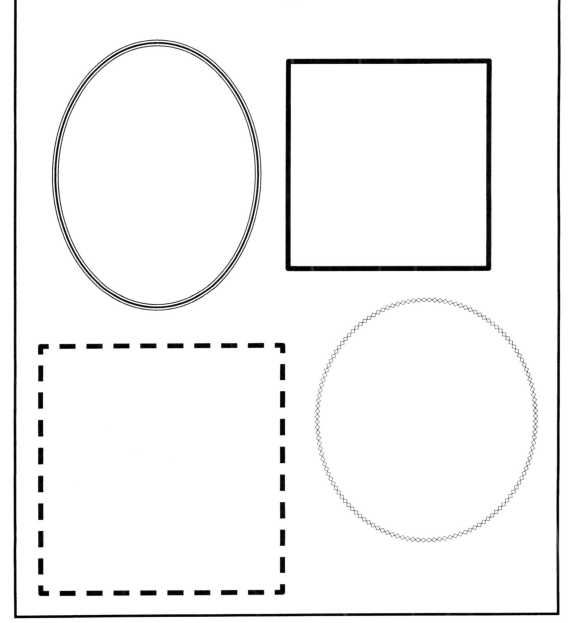

Remembering a Loved One

Sometimes we can celebrate a person's life by doing something very special like holding a big party or arranging a family outing that we know that person would have loved. What would you do to celebrate your special person?

Record you ideas below:

It's OK to be Happy

When someone we were close to has died it is sometimes hard to believe that we will ever feel happy again. Then, later on, when we do feel more like ourselves and laugh at a joke or feel happy, we can also feel guilty – as if it's not OK to be happy. Of course, it is OK, and the person that has died would be glad to think that we were feeling happier. Record some of the things that made you feel happy or feel like laughing. Use the smiley faces below.

Leave Me Alone!

Sometimes we need to take time out when we are feeling sad. This is OK – as long as we know that we can talk to others when we need to as well. Can you complete the sentences?

I need to be on my own when:

_____

_____

I like being on my own because:

_____

_____

When I'm on my own I feel:

_____

_____

When I'm on my own I think:

_____

_____

I know when I've been on my own for the right amount of time because:

_____

_____

When I need company I can find:

_____

_____

New Life

In the spring time everything seems to come alive and grow. Things change quickly and people often feel happier or more hopeful when they see all the new life around them.

Can you write a poem or record your thoughts at this time?

New Life...

Reaching Out

When we are feeling really sad, we can sometimes go into our own worlds and not want anyone else around us. Sometimes this doesn't help because we get more lonely, sad, and even depressed. We need to be able to reach out to others and to show them that we need them. We don't always need to talk. Sometimes we just need a hug or to spend some time watching TV with a friend or someone special. How can you reach out to others? Think of five strategies and write them out below:

1. I could _____

_____

_____

2. I could _____

_____

_____

3. I could _____

_____

_____

4. I could _____

_____

_____

5. I could _____

_____

_____

Look After Yourself
Stress Busters

When you're feeling sad, angry or stressed, it is important to help yourself by making use of some 'stress busters'. Put a tick next to the strategies you might use and then record some of your own.

- [ ] 1. Going for a run.
- [ ] 2. Listening to some music.
- [ ] 3. Having a bath.
- [ ] 4. Reading a funny book.
- [ ] 5. Jogging or jumping.
- [ ] 6. Painting a picture
- [ ] 7. Deep breathing.
- [ ] 8. Speaking to a friend
- [ ] 9. Thinking positive thoughts
- [ ] 10. Having a treat
- [ ] 11. Buying something new
- [ ] 12. Taking time out
- [ ] 13. Counting to ten or twenty
- [ ] 14. _____
- [ ] 15. _____
- [ ] 16. _____
- [ ] 17. _____
- [ ] 18. _____

Which three strategies work best for you and why?

Peaceful Places

When we are feeling really sad, stressed, angry or upset we can sometimes help ourselves by imagining that we are in a beautiful and peaceful place. It is best to do this in the peace of your room. Shut your eyes and drift away…what do you see? Draw your peaceful picture below:

My peaceful picture

Write About It

Whatever you feel – record it! When we are feeling sad, angry or very upset we sometimes can't deal with it straightaway. Sometimes we need to think about it and discuss it or deal with it afterwards. We can write our feelings down.

Scaling Activity 2

Try this scaling activity when you feel you will find it useful...

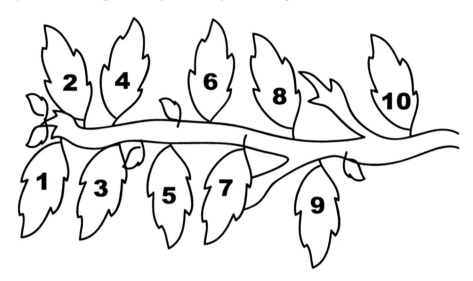

Where am I now?

_____

Why have I done to get to...?

_____

Where do I want to go next?

_____

How can I get there? What do I need to do?

_____

Who else can help me?

_____

How will I know when I've reached this point? What will
I feel like? What will be happening around me?

_____

Chapter Five

Books for Children

The following list of books is not exhaustive. It aims to provide some useful resources for those supporting children who are experiencing the pain of loss and bereavement. These books have been recommended to us by a range of educationalists and mental health workers who have supported young people through this process.

Bereavement

▸ Althea (1982) *When Uncle Bob Died*, Dinosaur Publications. Aimed at 5 to 8 year olds, this lovely book talks about fear, anger, sadness and memories.

▸ Blume, J. (1998) *Tiger Eyes*, Macmillian Books. This books tells the story of a boy who has to cope with intense feelings after the sudden and violent death of his father during a shop raid (Age 12 to 18)

▸ Burningham, J. (2003) *Granpa*. Puffin Books. With gentle, delicate illustrations Burningham tells of the bond between a girl and her grandfather. At the end there is his empty chair and we know he has died. This book gives an excellent basis for sharing ideas about loss and death in particular. (Age 4+)

▸ Dahl, R. (1967) *James and the Giant Peach*. Allen and Unwin. James lives with his awful aunts following the death of his parents who were eaten by an escaped rhinoceros. One day a spectacular peach begins to grow in the back garden. The book shows how the spirit to survive against all the odds, with the help of friends, carries James through his great adventure.

▸ Hessell, J. (1989) *Nobody's Perfect*, Hutchison. This is the story of a child who dies. At school his friends react in many ways to his death and the book shows how death can affect friends as well as family. A useful book to have in schools as a basis for discussion.

▶ Lewis, C. S. (1950) *The Lion, the Witch and the Wardrobe*, Geoffrey Bles. This classic book works well on so many levels that children are enchanted by it. The death of Aslan and the spiritual dimension of the story make it particularly pertinent in exploring loss.

▶ Magorian, M. (1983) *Goodnight Mr Tom*, Penguin. As an evacuee from London Will discovers warmth and love in the care of Mr Tom. This brilliant book incorporates many aspects of loss from physical abuse, rejection by his mother and death yet remains a story full of hope and trust regained.

▶ Mystrom, C. (1990) *Emma Says Goodbye*, Lion Publishing Series. Aunty Sue is young, strong and lively. Emma finds her way of coming to terms with Sue's illness and death (12+).

▶ Paterson, K. (1995) *Bridge To Terbaitha*, Puffin. This is the story of a friendship between two ten year olds. When one dies in an accident, the other has to manage her feelings of grief and loss. (7-12)

▶ Simmonds, P. (1989) *Fred*, Puffin Books. A wonderfully told story of the death of a cat and his amazing funeral with characteristically quirky illustrations.

▶ Simms, A. (1986) *Am I Still A Sister?* Slidell, LA. Big A and Co. This thoughtful book written by a young person following her baby brother's death, addresses a whole range of emotions and situations following the death of a sibling.

▶ Smith, D. B. (1987) *A Taste of Blackberries*, Penguin. A sensitive and sympathetic story. Telling of the death of a friend caused by an allergy to bee stings.

▶ Stickney, D. (1997) *Waterbugs and Dragonflies*, Mowbray. A book for younger children which gives a sensitive and straightforward explanation of death. It also deals with the idea of life after death and is a helpful way to introduce the concept of the life cycle. (Infants)

▶ Varley, S. (1994) *Badgers's Parting Gift*, Collins. A lovely book to help in looking at memories, what they mean and how they can help. The animals are able to come to terms with the death of Badger their friend in remembering all the things he had done. (5-11)

▶ Viorst, J. (1972) *The Tenth Good Thing About Barney*, Collins. Story of a young boy who is mourning the death of his cat.

▶ White, E.B. (1993) *Charlotte's Web*. Puffin. This classic story relates the powerful relationship between Wilber the pig and Charlotte the spider. It beautifully describes the life cycle and the power of love and acceptance in a readily accessible way. (7-12)

Separation and divorce

▸ Blume, J. (1992) *It's Not The End Of the World,* Del Publishing Company. Eleven year old Grainne said, 'I once dreamt that I was Karen in Judy Blume's 'It's Not The End of the Word. This confused me but prepared me too. Karen's parents were splitting up and it shows what troubles they went through'.

▸ Brown, L. K. & Brown, M. (1987) *Dinosaurs Divorce: A Guide For Changing Families*, Collins. The authors, both divorced themselves, present different aspects of divorce as seen through a child's eyes. Aimed at children under ten, it has delightful pictures accompanying a sensitive test to describe the uncomfortable emotions raised by divorce including fear and anger. It provides an easy way to talk about divorce through the events that happen in dinosaur land.

▸ Fine, A. (1999) *Google Eyes*, Read - Along. Kitty is coming to terms with changes in her Mum and her new suitor. Lots of vitality and an ingenious ending. Great Fun. (9+)

▸ Nystrom, C. (1991) *Mike's Lonely Summer.* The Lion Care Series. This child's guide to divorce is sensible and down to earth. Like others in this series by the same author, each book combines a story with boxes of information, question and comment.

▸ Wilson, J. (1995) *Double Act*, Doubleday. Ten-year-old identical twins Ruby and Garnet do everything together, especially since their mother died three years earlier. The new woman in their father's life is certainly spooked by their double act. Loss and forming new relationships are central themes in this delightful book.

Illness

▸ Bales, H. (1987) *What's Up Mate?* Hodder and Stoughton. A book specially written for children between five and twelve, who have been recently diagnosed with cancer or leukemia to help them learn about their illness and its treatment.

▸ Bergman, T. (1989) *One Day At A Time: Children Living With Leukemia* Gareth Steven's Children's Books. Actual photographs of children in hospital accompanying their stories. It includes questions from children, such as 'What is cancer?' 'What is the treatment for leukemia?' It gives simple straightforward answers.

▸ Gillespie, J. (1989) *Brave Heart: The Diary of a nine year old girl who refused to die,* Century London. Joanne's delightful illustrations accompany her text. "I decided to write this book,' she says 'because when I was frightened and not sure myself in hospital there was nothing for me to read. There were books for grown-ups but there were none for children. So, I decided to write this book for other children who are like me feeling frightened and ill. I hope it will help them to feel a bit more sure of themselves."

▶ Dixon, P. (1991) *AIDS and you*, Kingsway Publications. Mainly aimed at young children who know someone with AIDS.

▶ LeBlanc, S, (1999) *A Dragon in Your Heart*, Jessica Kingsley Publishers. This illustrated text describes how Sophie explained to her five-year-old daughter about the fact that she had cancer. Designed to explain to younger children the nature of the illness in a sensitive and accessible way.

▶ Reuter, E. (1989) *Christopher's Story,* Hutchison. A beautifully illustrated story about a boy with leukemia. Gentle and sensitive story for junior age range children.

Family relationships

▶ Houghton, E. (2000) *Rainy Day*, Doubleday. Illustrator Angelo Rinaldi captures the mood of a rainy day visit to his dad. Though there is nothing obvious for them to do Ned and his father make their way to the sea and eat biscuits. When father says, 'Rainy days don't last forever' you know it's a message of hope for both of them. (5+)

▶ Hughes, S. (1983) *Alfie Lends A Hand*. Bodley Head. Alfie lives with his baby sister and his mum. Very well illustrated, it tells of the time Alfie goes to his first birthday party and takes his old blanket 'comforter' with him to help him get over his fear of being away from his mum. (3-6)

▶ McAfee, A. (2000) *The Visitors Who Came to Stay*, Walker Books. Katy lives alone with her father and has mixed feelings about the arrival of Mary and her son Sean. Katy learns that it is possible to grow fond of people you thought were your enemies. Bold, entrancing illustrations. (5+)

Abuse

▶ Elliot, M. (1993) *The Willow Street Kids: It's Your Right To Be Safe*, Macmillan's Children's Books. This fictionalised account for older primary school children of actual events of attempted abuse as told by two girls, includes the approach of 'The Stranger' and how to deal with the 'bad secret' of unwanted attentions from an uncle. Good fiction and healthy, empowering message for children.

▶ Howard, E. (1987) *Gillyflower*, Collins. A moving story about a twelve-year-old girl's experience of sexual abuse by her father. She realises that she has to take action that might damage the family in order to repair her life. It shows the complexities of the situation and just how trapped someone in Gilly's position can be. (12+)

General

▸ Coppard, Y. (1990) *Bully*, Bodley Head. The hero Kerry is crippled after an accident and dramatically tackles the boy who teases and bullies her. His secret gives her the key!

▸ Mathews, A. (2000) *Stiks and Stoans,* Mammoh. Ella, the victim of bullying is dyslexic and overweight. Through diary entries her experiences at the hands of a group of bullies are described and interspersed with narration by Liam, a new boy at the school. It addresses the desire to gain the acceptance of peers at the expense of someone else's unhappiness. Good basis for discussion work.

▸ Ashworth, S. (2000) *What's Your Problem?* Livewire. Jac is a confident teenager in the middle of her GCSEs when she has to move schools. The intensity of bullying by the girls at the new school shows how confidence crumbles and cruelty intensifies until she is forced to take action.

▸ Holm, A. (1979), *I Am David*, Methuen. Prize winning fiction for older readers, this book is about a boy who escapes from a camp during World War Two and tramps his way across Europe searching for his identity and a family. Full of hope and tenderness.

▸ Frank, A. (1954), *The Diary of Anne Frank*, Pan. Anne Frank wrote her diary in hiding from Nazi terror in an Amsterdam attic from 1942 to 1944, when she was aged between thirteen and fifteen. As a beacon of hope in the darkest times it portrays adolescent hope and fears in the face of great loss.

▸ McEwan, I. (1985), *Rose Blanche*, Jonathan Cape. Delightful illustrations intensify the tragedy of this story in which Rose, seeing the changes in her small German village, gradually becomes aware of what is happening to the people the army takes away. The dawning of the horrifying truth brings home the message of how innocence is destroyed by the brutality of war. Beautifully written.

▸ Nain, S. and Speed, M. (1999), *Dad's in Prison,* A & C Black. A book that is sensitively illustrated with photographs all about two boys' first visit to their father who is in prison.

Useful Addresses

Childline

2nd Floor Royal Mail Building

Studd Street

London N1 0QW

Tel: 020 7359 9392

National Children's Bureau

8, Wakely Street

London EC 1V

Tel: 020 7843 6000

NCH Action for Children

85, Highbury Park

London N5 1ND

Tel: 020 7226 2033

The Children's Society

Edward Rudolf House

Margery Street

London WC1X 0JL

Tel: 020 7837 4299

National Council for One Parent Families

255 Kentish Town Road

London NW5 2LX

Tel: 020 7267 1361

Federation of Prisoner's Families Support Group

c/o SCF, Cambridge House

Cambridge Grane

London W6 OLE

Tel: 020 8741 4578

Step Family

72, Willsden Lane

London NW6 7TA

Tel: 020 7372 0844

Orniston Children and Families Trust

333 Felixstowe Road

Ipswich

Suffolk IP3 9BU

Tel: 01473 724517

Carers National Association

20 – 25 Glanhouse

London EC1A 4JS

Tel: 020 7490 8818

Crossroads UK

10 Regent Place

Rugby CU21 2PN

Tel: 0788 573 653

Young Carers Research Group

Department of Social Service

Loughborough University

Tel: 0509 223379

The Refugee Council

3 Bondway

London SW8 1SJ

Tel: 020 7820 3000

Bereavement

The Alder Centre

Royal Liverpool Children's Hospital

Alder Hey

Liverpool L12 2AP

Tel: 0151 252 5513 / Child Death Helpline 0800 282 986

Offers support to anyone who has been affected by the death of a child. Volunteers and trained counsellor provide help for adults and children. A telephone helpline is available.

Bereaved Parents Helpline

6 Cannon's Gate

Harlow

Essex

Tel: 0129 412745

The Child Bereavement Trust

Brindley House

4 Burkes Road

Beaconsfield

Bucks

Tel: 01494 678088

Support on all aspects of bereavement involving children

The Compassionate Friend

6 Denmark Street

Bristol BS1 5DQ

This self-help, national organisation offers support to anyone who has lost a child. There are two sub-groups, one for parents of murdered children and one for parents of suicide victims. They also have an extensive library from which you may borrow books and tapes.

Cruse – Bereavement Care

Cruse House

126 Sheen Road

Richmond

Surrey TW9 1UR

Tel: 020 8940 4818

Gay Bereavement Project

Unitarian Rooms

Hoop Lane

London NW11 8BS

Tel: 020 8455 8894

Institute of Family Therapy

43 New Cavendish Street

London W1M 7RG

The Institute's Elizabeth Raven Memorial Fund offers free counselling to recently bereaved families or those with seriously ill family members. They work with the whole family.

Winston's Wish

Gloucestershire Royal Hospital

Great Western Road

Gloucester GL1 3NN

Tel: 01452 394377

Email: info@winstonswish.org.uk

Website: www.winstonswish.org.uk

The national charity offers a grief support programme for children. It gives children and families the chance to meet others who have experienced bereavement on a 'Camp Winston' residential course. This inspirational organisation also offers ongoing support, training, telephone advice and leaflets.

Citizen's Advice Bureaux

Give information and advice on matters related to death including funeral arrangements and disposal of possessions.

Divorce and Separation

Mediation and Conciliation Services

The National Family Conciliation Council

Shaftesbury Avenue

Percy Street

Swindon SN2 2AZ

National Council for One Parent Families

255 Kentish Town Road

London NW5 2LX

Seeks to improve conditions for one parent families and offers advice to families in need of help

Stepfamily – The National Step family Association

162 Tennison Road

Cambridge CB1 2DP

Offers practical help, support and information to all members of stepfamilies.

Illness

ACT (Association for Children with Life Threatening Conditions and Their Families)

Institute of Child Health

Royal Hospital for Sick Children

St Michael's Hill

Bristol BS2 8BJ

National Resource and Information Service available to help with all aspects of life threatening illness in childhood.

BACUP

121/123 Charterhouse Street

London EC1M 6AA

Tel: 0800 181 199

Helps patients, their families and friends cope with cancer. Trained cancer nurses provide information, emotional support and practical advice by telephone or letter.

Cancer and Leukemia in Childhood Trust (CLIC)

Clic House

11-12 Freemantle Square

Cotham

Bristol BS6 5TL

Tel: 01179 244333

Offers information and support to children and families.

National Eczema Society

Tavistock House East

Tavistock Square

London WC1H 9SR

As many children suffer from eczema at times of stress, and as children with severe eczema may have special needs at school, this society have provided guidelines to assist. It is called 'A Practical Guide To The Management of Eczema in Schools', which includes tips for parents and school staff and is available from the above address.

National Association for the Welfare of Children in Hospital

Argyle House

29 – 31 Euston Road

London NW1 2SD

Advice on any matter relating to children in hospital.

The Malcolm Sargent Cancer Fund for Children

14 Abingdon Road

London W8 6AF

Can provide cash grants for parents of children with cancer to help pay for clothing, equipment, travel etc. Applications through a hospital social worker who will fill in a form on the patient's behalf. Available anywhere in the UK.

Mental Health Organisation – Young Minds – The Children's Mental Health Charity

102-108 Clerkenwell Road

London EC1M 5SA

Tel: 020 7336 8445

Email: young.minds@ukonline.co.uk

Website: youngminds.org.uk

A children's mental health charity which offers information and advice for anyone with concerns about the mental health of a child or young person.

References

Bowlby, J (1980) *Loss, Sadness and Depression. Basic Books*

Brown, E (1999), *Loss, Change and Grief: An Educational Perspective.* David Fulton.

Durkin, C, Warner, R and Sharkey, K (2001) *Children's Experiences of Separation and Loss.* Information for teachers London: Tower Hamlets Educational Psychology Service.

Dyregor, A (1990) *Grief in Children: A handbook for adults.* London: Jessica Kingsley.

Gatliffe, E (1988) *Death in the Classroom: A Resource Book for Teachers and Others.* Epworth Press.

Jewett, C (1982), *Helping Children Cope with Separation and Loss.* Batsford Academic.

Mallon, B (1998), *Managing Loss, Separation and Bereavement – Best Policy and Practice.* Manchester Education Matters.

McCarthy, S (1988), *A Death in the Family: a self-help guide to coping with grief.* Self Counsel Press.

Mitchell, L (1987), *International Stress and Tension Control.* Annual conference

Pincus, L (1976), *Death and the Family: The Importance of Mourning.* London. Faber and Faber.

Plant, S and Stoate, P (1989), *Loss and Change: Resources for use in Personal and Social Education Programme.* Crediton Southgate Publishers.

Raphael, B (1984), *The Anatomy of Bereavement: A handbook for the Caring Professions.* Unwin Hyman.

Rushton, L (1992) *Understanding Religions: Death Customs.* Wayland Press

Wagner, P (1993) *Children and Bereavement, Death and Loss: What can the school do?* Coventry National Association for Pastoral Care in Education.

Ward, B (1995), *Good Grief: Talking and Learning about Loss and Death with Under 11's.* Jessica Kingsley Publishers.

Wells, R (1988) *Helping Children Cope with Grief.* London: Sheldon Press.

Yule, W and Gold, A (1993) *Wise Before the Event.* Calouste Gulbenkian Foundation.

Don't forget to visit our website for all our latest publications, news and reviews.

New publications every year on our specialist topics:

- ▸ **Emotional Literacy**

- ▸ **Self-esteem**

- ▸ **Bullying**

- ▸ **Positive Behaviour Management**

- ▸ **Circle Time**

- ▸ **Anger Management**

- ▸ **Asperger's Syndrome**

- ▸ **Eating Disorders**

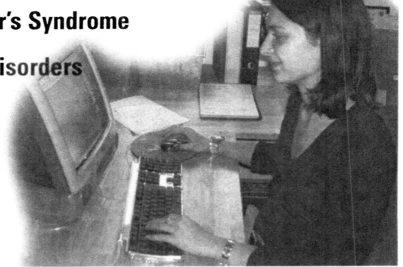

Lightning Source UK Ltd.
Milton Keynes UK
18 January 2011

165910UK00001B/85/P

9 781904 315421